CHANGING CAREERS

CHANGING CAREERS

HOW TO MAKE A SUCCESSFUL CAREER CHANGE

PAUL GOODHEAD

LEADS PRESS
an imprint of
B. Jain Publishers (P) Ltd.
An ISO 9001 : 2000 Certified Company
USA — EUROPE — INDIA

CHANGING CAREERS—HOW TO MAKE A SUCCESSFUL CAREER CHANGE

First Indian Edition: 2007

Copyright © 2004 Paul Good head. All rights reserved. No part of this book may be used or reproduced in any manner whatsoever without written permission except in the case of brief quotations embodied in critical articles or reviews.

Published in India by
Kuldeep Jain
for

LEADS PRESS

an imprint of **B. Jain Publishers (P) Ltd.**
An ISO 9001 : 2000 Certified Company
1921, Street No. 10, Chuna Mandi,
Paharganj, New Delhi 110 055 (INDIA)
Phones: 91-11-2358 0800, 2358 1100, 2358 1300
Fax: 91-11-2358 0471; *Email:* bjain@vsnl.com
Website: **www.bjainbooks.com**

Printed in India by
J.J. Offset Printers
522, FIE, Patpar Ganj, Delhi - 110 092
Phones: 91-11-2216 9633, 2215 6128

ISBN: 81-8056-812-1

BOOK CODE: BG-5941

CONTENTS

Introduction   7

Chapter 1: The big picture   11
Life cycle of a job – When to think about job shifting –
A framework for thinking about job satisfaction – An approach
to planning for career success – Obstacles to be faced

Chapter 2: Where have you been? Where are you now?   22
Career lifeline – career drivers – individual values –
transferable skills – skills versus strengths – creating a skills
inventory – assessing likes, tolerables and dislikes

Chapter 3: What would you really like to do?   37
Future of work – work versus jobs – creating a personal
vision – alternative processes – first steps

Chapter 4: Upgrading your skills   49
Lifetime learning – learning needs – training versus
non-training needs – skills and strengths – permission
to use a skill – training options – training plans – finding
the time

Chapter 5: Dealing with obstacles and constraints   59
Anxieties – types of obstacles – fixed constraints – tactics
to handle obstacles – substitute factors – potential losses
in career changes – managing risk

Chapter 6: Pulling it together: creating the plan   70
    List of tasks – timetabling – short-term actions and first steps – Plan B – keeping motivation – knowing-doing gap

Chapter 7: Job seeking   81
    Where are the jobs? – job content – marketing yourself – networking and visibility – CVs and interviews – self-employment – managing stress

Chapter 8: Making the move   95
    Forcefield analysis – motivators – enjoying the journey

INTRODUCTION

At least once, somewhere between the ages of 30 and 55, you are likely to look at your job or career and ask yourself: *Do I want to do this for the rest of my working life?* Maybe you have 'proved yourself' in your current role and the challenge has stopped. Maybe you just don't enjoy what you are doing any more, or the toll it takes on other aspects of your life is too high.

The next question, then, is: *What else would I do?* Many people get stuck at this point, especially those who have been successful in a particular field to date. 'This is all I know how to do,' they say.

And the third consideration is: *If I did make a change, I have a lot to lose. I would probably step backwards in terms of income or skill/experience. How would I manage that?*

This book helps you to answer those three questions and make successful mid-life career decisions. It presents frameworks to clarify your thinking, practical tools and processes to create your plan and ideas for when you get stuck.

You could probably read the contents of this book straight through in a couple of evenings. But as the essayist and US Supreme Court judge Oliver Wendell Holmes once said, 'It is a good reader that makes the book', so you may want to dwell on some ideas that strike you as important or that unsettle your thinking. The chapters are short so you can stop frequently. Take a walk in the park. Talk to friends and family. Play with the suggested exercises.

Yes, *play*. Career planning is as much creative and intuitive activity

Changing Careers

as it is a logical exercise. But this is serious play. So, as your ideas crystallise, write down your thoughts so that you do not lose them.

Inertia is a common mid-career problem. There are probably a lot of ties to your current occupation and a number of potential risks and uncertainties if you make a move. So it is easy to procrastinate. This book aims to facilitate forward momentum. Its goals are simple:

- ✔ To give you a set of concepts for clarifying your ideas about future career changes;

- ✔ To give you some practical techniques and processes to get there;

- ✔ To help you motivate yourself to get started and keep moving in the right direction.

The structure of the book follows a logical sequence:

Chapter 1 gives the big picture of career concepts and processes;

Chapter 2 gets you to explore your career history to learn lessons about your likes and dislikes and to inventory the skills in your repertoire;

Chapter 3 helps you to clarify what you want in your future work.

These three chapters should be read first, in sequence. The rest of the book then concentrates on how to bring your future dreams into reality. Although the chapters are written in the most sensible order (as described below), a lot of the tasks you need to think about interweave. So you could read the chapters in a different order if you want, and you will want to refer backwards and forwards to refine your career thinking and planning as you go.

Introduction

Chapter 4 deals with identifying the skills you need to upgrade and the methods of doing this;

Chapter 5 recognises that there are obstacles and constraints attached to career shifting. These are explored so that you can devise tactics so that obstacles don't stop you progressing;

Chapter 6 works on creating your career plan;

Chapter 7 is about implementing that plan and it covers some specifics about approaches to job search and job winning;

Finally, Chapter 8 summarises the key considerations and helps you to marshal your resources for your career adventure.

The philosophy presented in these pages is that insightful thinking helps you formulate better plans. But plans need to be practical to be implemented. So the 'real world' needs to be balanced against the 'ideal'. And finally — and most importantly — *actions* need to follow to bring about *change*.

Chapter 1

THE BIG PICTURE

Key ideas in this chapter:
- Life Cycle of a job
- When to think about job shifting
- A framework for thinking about Job Satisfaction
- An approach to planning for Career Success
- Obstacles to be faced

This chapter sets out the conceptual framework for the whole book. Ensuing chapters look into the 'how to' details, but the ideas put forward here are designed to start you thinking. So let's get straight into the first idea.

LIFE CYCLE OF A JOB

Diagram 1 on page 12 illustrates the Life Cycle of a job in terms of how your levels of comfort and competence (vertical axis) change the longer you spend in a job (horizontal axis). It is an oversimplification of the relationship, but you should recognise what it expresses:

Changing Careers

- ✔ When you are new to a job, anxiety may be high but comfort starts to increase as you build competence — you are on the *upward* slope.

- ✔ When you reach full competence, comfort and satisfaction are high because you are skilled, you obtain results, you get positive feedback and hopefully you receive appropriate rewards — you are on the *plateau*.

- ✔ However, if you stay in the job too long you start to get stale — you are on the *downward* slope. How long is too long? The answer to this question will vary from job to job and person to person.

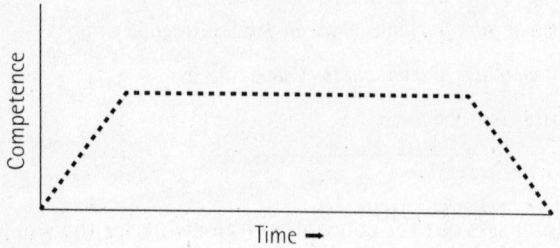

Diagram 1: Profile of a job

You may have already worked out where you are on this model in respect to your current job. If you have not, take a moment to think about it now.

TIMING IS EVERYTHING

Now, here is a key question: At what position on this graph should you begin thinking about your next job change?

Unfortunately, many people neglect this consideration until they are on the downward slope. Obviously, this is too late. Motivation and performance may have started to wane, damaging both your reputation and your confidence.

People who find themselves in this situation often move to escape from a bad job rather than progress towards a good one. It is a major reason why you see some people bounce through say seven jobs in ten years.

The point at which you should think seriously about future career options is when you are on the second half of the high plateau. But why think about moving when you are enjoying your work? In that sense, a move seems counterintuitive, even if you accept that this is the right time to consider one.

Nor is it an easy matter to predict when exactly you will reach the end of the plateau and start the descent. Furthermore, jobs do not always stay static; they can evolve in ways that introduce fresh stimulation and interest and prolong the duration of plateau.

YOU HAVE THREE CHOICES

Notwithstanding such reservations, the inescapable truth about the competence/time model is that there are only three future routes from the plateau:

- The first option is to stay and wait for the eventual decline. Bad news!
- The second option is to find a new job.
- The third option is to reinvent the current job.

The second and third options are both proactive, and are more likely

Changing Careers

to be successful if you have a clear insight into what you want to move towards, rather than what you want to leave behind.

To help you clarify this insight, let's turn to our next model.

JOB SATISFACTION

Diagram 2 is adapted from an idea developed by Paul Stevens, one of Australia's foremost experts on career planning. It illustrates the concept of Job Satisfaction in very simple terms. Job Satisfaction is the area in which the three circles — what you enjoy, what you are good at, and what the job needs — overlap; the greater the overlap, the greater the degree of satisfaction.

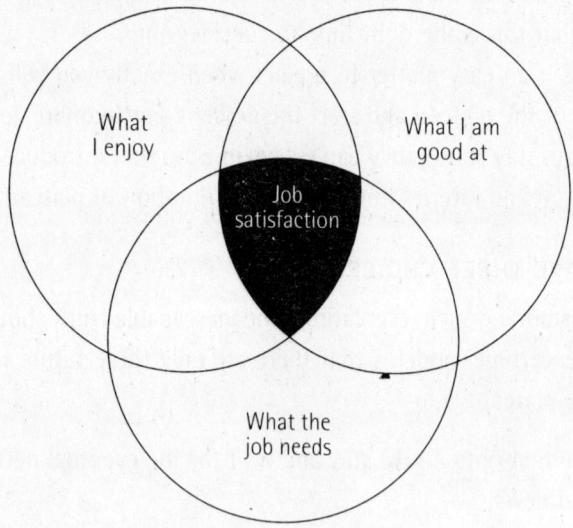

Diagram 2: Model of Job Satisfaction

In other words, you derive Job Satisfaction from doing things where:

☑ you are good at doing them, and

The big picture

- ✓ you enjoy doing them, and
- ✓ someone is willing to pay you to do them.

All three of these conditions must be met for a satisfying job. Two out of three is not good enough. So:

- If you are good at it and you enjoy it, but no one will pay you for doing it, then you have a satisfying hobby.
- If you are good at it and paid for it, but you don't enjoy doing it, then you have a drudge task or job.
- If you enjoy it and you are paid for it, but you don't do it well, then you are an endangered species!

So you need to maximise the overlap between your three circles. The good news is that two of your circles can be moved. The bad news is that the third cannot.

If you are not good at something, then you can get training (or coaching, or experience et cetera). Clearly there are some practical limits to an individual's trainability or potential, but there is always scope for you to adjust your 'good at' circle.

The 'job needs' circle can also be moved — within reasonable limits. For example, you can choose which jobs you apply for, how you market yourself and what other positioning and job search techniques you use. Of course, there is no point in applying for a job which is well beyond your capability, experience and trainability. But equally, there is no point in constraining yourself to jobs which bore you but which you just happen to be qualified to do. Choose your job search approach to maximise the overlap with your other two circles.

The circle least available for manipulation is the 'enjoy' circle. Its scope will evolve over time, but you cannot really direct it. For instance, deciding that 'Tomorrow I am going to enjoy filing or go on a course to teach me to enjoy filing' just won't happen!

Your 'enjoy' circle is influenced by your internal motivators and preferences, the values you hold dear, and a range of other psychological considerations that you may or may not be consciously aware of. These factors will be looked at in more detail in subsequent chapters.

THE WRONG AND RIGHT WAYS TO PLAN A CAREER

Here is where most people go about career planning from the wrong direction. They start by looking at the job adverts ('job needs'). Then they assess how much of a particular job specification they are capable of doing ('good at'). Finally, they hope that they will enjoy it because they are doing things they are good at.

They may be right or lucky. *Maybe.*

A far more reliable approach is to start from the other end. Since your likes and dislikes are fairly fixed, work these out first (there are processes outlined in the following chapters to help you do this). You need to figure out your preferences for the future in terms of the skills that you have that you want to use, the skills that you would like to acquire, and the employment setting in which you want to employ these skills.

Next, you need to assess your current level of competence in these preferred areas and put together a plan to boost your competence in the important ones.

Finally, you need to search for the ideal job or jobs — or create them.

In this way you are drawing the two moveable circles closer

towards the fixed one. In other words, you are managing your career rather than have it manage you.

Career Success

'But it's not that easy,' you might be saying at this point (you're right — this would be a very short book if it were).

The formula below expresses one of the more significant complications you will encounter:

$$CS = M + V + S - O$$

CS stands for Career Success — the more the better.

M stands for your internal Motivators (we will explore these in Chapter 3).

V stands for the values you want to incorporate into your work life.

S stands for the skills that you prefer to use in your work.

Collectively, **M**, **V** and **S** constitute your vision for your ideal career. The more of each of these factors that you can satisfy in your work, the more your sense of career success will be enhanced.

Incidentally, neither career nor job satisfaction necessarily imply climbing up the corporate ladder or chasing promotions. Some careers grow *upward*. Others grow *outward* (via broadening your range of experiences). Others grow *inward* (by deepening your intrapersonal experiences). The right path for *you* depends on *your* preferences, not on some external notion of what constitutes a successful career.

O represents the obstacles in your way. The minus sign before it means that the more obstacles you confront, the less your likelihood of career success. Unfortunately, the real world throws up numerous obstacles for all of us. These include:

- physical limitations of your body;
- geographical limitations of where you live;
- financial needs and obligations;
- educational and emotional factors;
- family and social considerations.

We will explore these specific obstacles in Chapter 5.

Some obstacles are perpetual and some are short term. Some are imposed on you and some are a result of choices that you make. Some are real and some are perceived.

You cannot ignore these obstacles, but neither should they run your life. Unfortunately, for some people, *managing* the obstacles becomes their career plan rather than just something that needs to be *factored in* to the plan.

A major obstacle for mid-career people yearning for a new start can be letting go of their current occupation. If you have invested a lot to get where you are now, and particularly if you are very successful, then you may feel that you will be sacrificing a good deal to move on to something new.

If your sense of loss is too great, you may be better off staying in your current occupation. But take another look at Diagram 1 first. Only *you* can judge whether you are making a balanced, pragmatic choice or just delaying the inevitable.

But if you do decide that you need to move and you recognise that there are major obstacles in your path, then there are two things you can do to help you make the transition:

The big picture

1. Develop a plan to eliminate, minimise, circumvent or manage your obstacles.

2. Formulate really clear and strong ideas about your personal motivators, values and skills. In other words, make sure that the M, V and S positives significantly outweigh the O negatives in your formula for Career Success.

That is the essence of what you will be reading about and working on in the following chapters.

SUMMARY

This chapter introduced a number of key concepts underpinning successful career planning.

The 'Life Cycle' idea identified predictable stages of any job and the way you feel about it. The best time for career action is when you are enjoying the job and successful at performing it, not when you are bored and in danger of decline.

The 'Job Satisfaction' model demonstrated that your preferences (what you enjoy) should drive your career choices, not the vacancy listings. The planning sequence is:

☆ Work out your vision in terms of the skills and values that you want to incorporate in your future work;

☆ Create a self-development plan to acquire/improve key skills and experience;

☆ Then, conduct the job search to match your specifications.

Finally, the 'Career Success' equation identified that there are numerous obstacles to contend with. These obstacles will derail your career plan unless you deal with them.

ENDNOTE

Back at the beginning of this chapter, you were invited to identify where you are now on Diagram 1. The ideal is that you are on the high plateau. It is possible, though, that you already see yourself on the slippery slope. If the latter is the case, all is not lost, but you face some additional challenges.

The first thing to realise is that you no longer have a choice but to be proactive. If you do nothing, the trend will continue to track downwards and any opportunity to influence the consequences may eventually be out of your hands. Nor is it a good idea to leave your current job without a positive alternative lined up.

Depending on how far down the slope you are, recognise that your negotiating power is weaker than it was and you need to restore that power before you can access better career choices.

Personal pride may have safeguarded you against letting your standards of work slip, but there may be other ways in which your attitude, cooperation or motivation has ebbed. Often, others can see this and react negatively.

If your motivation, performance and attitude have suffered, then it is unlikely that a competent manager would be willing to reinvent your job. They would not want to reward you with more interesting work if you were seen to be neglecting your current duties. Nor would your chances be high of getting a good reference if you sought to leave at this point. So you could find yourself locked into the downward trajectory.

It makes sense that they won't help you until you help yourself. In other words, you cannot control what they do, but you can control what you do.

The big picture

First you need to marshal your self-discipline to get your performance, motivation and attitude consistently up to the 'competent performer' level. If you have let things slip, pull them back up. If you have done it before, you can do it now, for the short term at least.

Put aside any feelings of being treated unfairly, undervalued, mistreated, degraded or whatever other negatives you may feel. They may be valid reactions but they are not useful.

Your motivation for this sort of self-discipline may not come easily, but it arises out of a singular vision: to get out of here to a better life. Use that vision to drive you to perform until you have created some new choices.

Of course, in parallel you can do the planning tasks outlines in this book to help you clarify what you really want, but you will be unlikely to be able to fully implement your plan until you have bolstered your current position.

When the evidence is clear that you can and do perform well, then you are in a position to either secure a new job or negotiate from a position of strength for changes to your current job to revitalise it.

CHAPTER 2

WHERE HAVE YOU BEEN? WHERE ARE YOU NOW?

Key ideas in this chapter:
- *Career Lifeline*
- *Career Drivers*
- *Individual Values*
- *Transferable Skills*
- *Skills versus Strengths*
- *Creating a Skills Inventory*
- *Assessing Likes, Tolerables and Dislikes*

People learn by *doing*, right?

Wrong. People learn by doing then *reflecting* on what they did: what worked; what didn't; what to repeat or change for next time.

So you will start the career thinking journey by looking backwards at where you have been. The aim of this chapter is for you to establish a clear word-picture of your motivators, values, likes and dislikes. You will do that by examining your career journey so far.

Where have you been? Where are you now?

CAREER LIFELINE EXERCISE

Here is a simple exercise to start you off. Diagram 3 shows how it works (using my career as an example). It is called a lifeline and, basically, you are going to trace your career to date according to how satisfying it has been to you.

Start with a piece of paper and draw the axes of your lifeline. The horizontal axis lays out the time from the start of your career (on the left) through to today (on the right).

The vertical axis depicts your degree of satisfaction with your work at each point in time (upwards is 'happy'; downwards is 'sad'). The scale is unscientific, of course. Happiness is relative, but you should be able to assess periods during your career when you were 'more happy' or 'less happy'.

Now, draw your career line from left to right. If there were good and bad periods within a particular job, mark all the changes. Draw quickly. Your first instinct is likely to be more accurate than if you stop to think about each change too much. Amplify the vertical movement so that you can quickly see the variance in ups and

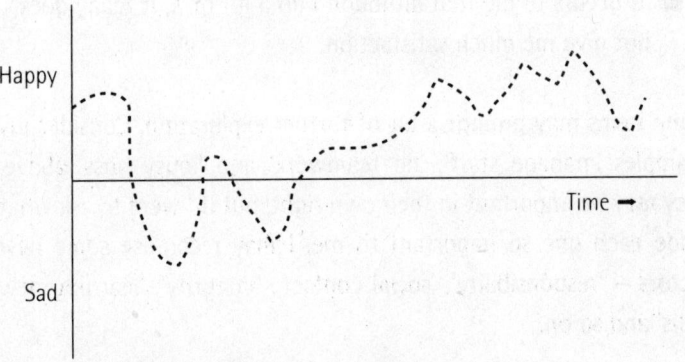

Diagram 3: Career Lifeline exercise

downs. Concentrate only on work happiness, not your life in general (you can do a similar exercise looking at your relationships, but that is another story).

The next task is to reflect on the line that you have drawn. Consider each of the peaks and troughs in turn, both major and minor. Write down some words or phrases that describe what made each point particularly good or bad for you. You may identify skill words (e.g. 'manage staff'), motivators met or unmet (e.g. 'given autonomy'; 'undervalued'), personal or organisational values (e.g. 'contributed to society'; 'no teamwork'), or other factors (e.g. 'lousy boss').

Now look back over your lists of words. The chances are, there are some words which repeat several times and there are themes which begin to emerge for you. Your aim now is to start to create a word-picture of your ideal job.

You may be able to make some statements, such as:

- ☑ 'These things are really important to me.'

- ☑ 'When these things feature in my work, I tend to be happier.'

- ☑ 'I would like to avoid too much of these things in my work.'

- ☑ 'It occurs to me that although I do a lot of X, it really does not give me much satisfaction.'

Some items may prompt a bit of further exploration. Consider my examples 'manage staff', 'no teamwork' and 'lousy boss' above. They may be important in their own right, but if I were to ask what made each one so important to me, I may recognise some new factors — 'responsibility', 'social contact', 'integrity', 'learning new skills' and so on.

Where have you been? Where are you now?

The more full the word-picture is, the more useful you will find it to be. Use the Career Lifeline exercise to spur other thinking about what you want and what you want to avoid in your work.

CAREER DRIVERS

Also known as Career Anchors, Career Drivers are the deep-seated motivators which endure through long periods of a person's life. If you are aware of your primary drivers and if you honour them in your job choices, then you are more likely to experience career happiness. If you ignore them or do not recognise them, then you may experience frustration or lack of fulfilment. Most people have one or two primary drivers.

Different writers use different models to describe the range of possible drivers. For example, MIT professor Edgar Schein lists eight:

- ☑ technical/functional competence
- ☑ managerial competence
- ☑ autonomy/independence
- ☑ security/stability
- ☑ entrepreneurialism/creativity
- ☑ service/dedication to a cause
- ☑ challenge
- ☑ lifestyle.

An older model which I use (so old that I cannot even recall the source) lists nine:

- ☑ material reward

- ☑ power and influence
- ☑ search for meaning
- ☑ expertise
- ☑ creativity
- ☑ affiliation and relationship
- ☑ autonomy
- ☑ security
- ☑ status.

You can see the overlaps between these models and that they also list some slightly different ideas. Identify the one or two which seem most to apply to you — as you actually are, not as the person you would wish you were. Adapt the lists if the headings do not feel quite right for you.

Now see if you can find evidence in your lifeline or your intuition to support your conclusions. Look for enduring parts of your worklife that you have tenaciously held on to and are reluctant to surrender. And look for times when you have been driven to do your best or to reach for something.

Recognise also that different people can approach the same job with different drivers. For example, one person may be attracted to a sales job in life insurance because of the link to material rewards coming from commission payments. Another may earn as much but value more the status that comes from being seen as top of the earnings league. Another may enjoy the autonomy or the lifestyle of working when and where they like. Another may enjoy helping people. Identical job, different drivers.

Where have you been? Where are you now?

I once worked with a chief executive who had sacrificed much over many years to fight his way to the top. Once there, he hated the job. What he realised too late was that he had spent half his lifetime chasing his father's career choices (he too had been a CEO), but both men had different drivers. A similar job, but one loved it and the other loathed it.

INDIVIDUAL VALUES

Drivers describe motivations or inner urges to do – to take action. Values, on the other hand, describe states of being and beliefs about what is right or wrong. Your values condition how you will behave.

Values run a spectrum from core, long-term beliefs (e.g. there is/is not a God) through to relatively day-to-day guides as to how you expect people to behave (e.g. swearing is bad). Values can also include some personal choices about how you choose to live your life (e.g. 'I believe in free speech'; 'I don't want to work nights'). Various writers have published numerous lists of values, though it is futile to try to list all the possibilities here. There are just too many.

Put in simple terms, if your work allows you to behave consistently with your important values, then you will feel happier and more whole. If you compromise your values, you can feel guilty, de-energised and dispirited. But your values may operate unconsciously within you unless you choose to bring them to the surface and examine them.

First list them, so you can then look for them in your work choices.

Here is a simple process for doing this:

1. Start by writing down those values that come obviously to mind as important to you.

2. Then use the following headings as prompts to spur you to think of other values that have meaning for you:
   - ☑ the ethics, motives and purpose of the organisation you prefer to work with;
   - ☑ the cultural norms and management style of the people within the organisation;
   - ☑ the relationship between your work and the rest of your life (e.g. family, friends, community and so on);
   - ☑ your own inner standards and ethics.

3. By now you will have a long wish list. However, not all of these values will be of equivalent strength or importance to you, so rank them now on a 5-point scale (5 = must have; 1 = nice to have).

4. As a further check, compare these words to the ones you applied to the peaks and troughs on your Career Lifeline exercise. Is a consistent picture emerging?

5. Finally, add the higher-ranked values to your emerging word-picture of your ideal work setting.

You may recognise in passing that some of the values that are important to you now are somewhat different from those you held dear earlier in your career. This is because values evolve as people evolve. Life stage, family circumstances, personal development, societal change: these all have an influence. The trick is not to lose touch with what is important to you. Yet it is very easy to lose

Where have you been? Where are you now?

connection when you are head down working to support yourself and your family and to advance your career.

Transferable Skills

Apparently the average person has over seven hundred transferable skills in their repertoire. 'Transferable skills' is career-speak for skills that can be applied in a variety of jobs and circumstances. Apparently, also, only about a quarter to a third of these skills are used in the workplace.

The accuracy of such statistics may be questioned, and there is a further problem in defining the size of a skill, but either way it points to a lot of untapped potential. When I have asked groups of people to list their skills, many dry up after about twenty items. The problem may be modesty, lack of imagination or lack of insight.

The inescapable conclusion is that most people have a lot more skills than they recognise or than they use. This skills-neglect is one of the main ways in which individuals limit their career choices more than anyone else does it for them.

Skills versus Strengths

A skill is simply the ability to do something.

Some people self-edit their skills lists because they do not feel that they do something better than everybody else. They confuse skills with strengths — and no employer would expect you to have seven hundred strengths. They want you to be competent at a lot of things and they may require you to be particularly competent in a handful of areas. If you have other strengths that you bring to the work, it may be a bonus and it helps you to stamp your individual mark on a piece of work.

For now though, you will just concentrate on identifying your skills. Later you can pinpoint which ones are strengths.

MINDMAPPING YOUR SKILLS

There are lots of methods for capturing your skills on paper to create your own personal Skills Inventory. Make lists. Brainstorm. Go through job adverts with a highlight marker identifying things that you can do (whether you are interested in the actual job ad is irrelevant). Keep pen and paper handy on your desk during the day, noting down each new skill as you use it.

Whatever method you use, it is crucial that you suspend judgement. Write everything down. You can edit out the dross later, but if you self-censor too early you will inhibit your insights and your imagination.

Perhaps the quickest and best way for many people to identify their skills is to use mindmapping. Mindmapping is a spacial way of capturing large numbers of ideas on paper in a short time. I have seen individuals identify 200+ skills for themselves in twenty minutes using this technique.

Diagram 4 shows the beginnings of a mindmap. Follow the procedures below to map one of your own.

1. Start by placing the central theme in the middle of your page ('My skills' in this case).

2. Work outwards identifying skills areas, giving each new theme a one- or two-word heading and its own space on the page. In this example, the themes identified were 'Work', 'Community', 'Family/homelife' and 'Hobbies'. These are useful headings that you could adopt, or you could choose your own themes. Do not feel constrained by a set structure.

Where have you been? Where are you now?

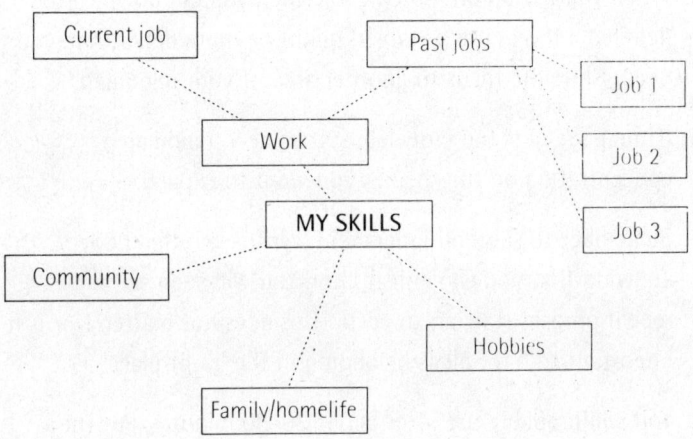

Diagram 4: The basics of a mindmap of skills

3. Shift your focus out to the second layer and develop each of these themes in turn. Again, use a word or phrase for each and spread them out so that they do not crowd each other. Avoid creating lists, because it will be hard to expand items in the middle of a list. The example I've presented has expanded 'Past jobs' to identify 'Job 1' etc. The lines between layers are useful to identify links, but do not worry if the page starts to look very messy. You can tidy up the ideas later when you extract them. For now, the more ideas the better.

4. Keep moving out, exploring each word or phrase to expand it. Job 1 would be expanded by identifying skills used in that job — for example 'interpersonal skills', 'typing', 'delegation', 'analysing data'. 'Interpersonal skills' could be further expanded to identify 'listening', 'questioning', 'negotiating' and so on.

5. When you dry up on a theme, or when you get down to too detailed a level ('use a stapler' might be more detail than you need), shift the focus to another area of your mindmap.

6. If the page gets too crowded, start a new mindmap concentrating on the themes you want to expand.

7. Remember to suspend judgement. Write everything down knowing that you can edit it later. You will soon see some repeat phrases starting to occur. This does not matter. Nor is it important to have ideas belonging in the 'right place'.

8. You will probably tire after about 20–30 minutes. Put the mindmap aside and come back to it later. Re-reading may spur new thoughts.

Some of the headings used as examples in Diagram 4 are interesting and important to explore further here.

Take 'Family/homelife' for example. You will recall the statistics about the relatively low proportion of your Transferable Skills that actually get used in your work. Well, it is in situations that come under the headings of Family, Hobbies and Community that all those other skills get used.

Consider, for example, the job of raising a family. This involves skills like time management, coaching, conflict resolution, budgeting, planning and juggling multiple projects, as well as the more mundane skills of cooking, cleaning and operating the family taxi service. Just because you do not always get paid for using a skill, does not mean that the skill does not matter.

This is one reason why this mindmapping exercise is particularly powerful for parents returning to the paid workforce after time out to rear children. It is not rare for such people (usually women) to underrate their skills and/or suffer from lower self-confidence because they 'haven't worked for a number of years'. Mindmapping helps them see the range of their skills and articulate the complexities of those abilities.

There is still the small problem of convincing a potential employer to value a skill acquired and applied in a non-paid setting. That will be covered in Chapter 7.

USING YOUR SKILLS INVENTORY

Once you have identified a good number of skills, there are several useful ways in which you can explore the list/mindmap further. You may want to make several photocopies of your workings so that you can use a different copy for each of the following tasks:

1. Even though you have up to seven hundred skills, you probably have some favourites and some you do not enjoy. Shortly you will assess your likes and dislikes. Remember the immovable circle ('What I enjoy') in Diagram 2 in Chapter 1.

2. Later, in Chapter 4, you will pull out those skills which constitute your strengths. You will also identify some other skills that you would like to turn into strengths.

3. Finally, you can compare your list to actual work opportunities (see Chapter 7). This will help you to realistically assess your suitability and identify any training and development needs that you should address. It may also ultimately help with presenting yourself via CV or face to face.

Assessing your Likes, Tolerables and Dislikes

It is now time to start editing and applying your judgement to your Skills Inventory. Take three highlighter marker pens in different colours — perhaps red, yellow and green.

Using the green pen, highlight all the words or phrases which identify skills that you would *like* to see used in any future work you do. These may be skills you have used in the past, or that you use now and want to continue to use or use more, or skills you use outside of work and that you would now like to include in your paid work. You may also think of new skills outside your repertoire that you would like to use. Add them in, then highlight them.

The yellow pen is for skills you will *tolerate* in your job but may not choose to seek.

The red pen is for those you *dislike* and want to eliminate. Be careful how many reds you allow yourself. It is easy on paper to cross out all the boring, menial or unpleasant stuff such as filing or attending meetings. In reality, all jobs have some bad bits, so you may be limiting your opportunities if you get too choosy.

Save the red pen for those few things that you really want to avoid, or keep to an absolute minimum in your work. You may then end up with more in the yellow. One of your goals is to make sure you do not end up in an occupation where you are spending a very high proportion of your time and energy on yellow tasks and skills.

How much green, yellow and red now?

Think about your current work. In rough percentages, how much time do you spend on work you like, dislike or just tolerate? Compare your conclusions to your rightmost mark on the timeline you drew in Diagram 3. To what degree does that explain your current level of happiness/unhappiness?

Incidentally, sometimes this analysis is just what you need to direct you to reinvent the job you are presently in by making minor adjustments, as opposed to making a complete job or career shift.

SUMMARY

This chapter involved a number of exercises to help you review your past to identify key considerations for you in your future career choices. These considerations included:

☆ Your Career Drivers: the one or two key motivators which sit at the heart of your sense of happiness and fulfilment.

☆ Your Values: your beliefs about what is right or wrong for you or for others in the environment in which you work. Your values condition how you will behave.

☆ Your Skills: the repertoire of things that you can do. Your aim is to use more of the skills that you like and fewer of those that you do not like.

Collectively, all this information forms a word-picture about you and your preferences for future work. It needs drawing together into a succinct form. You will do that in the next chapter.

It also needs to pass two later tests: is it realistic and is it practical? Only you can judge this, but a couple of later chapters will help you make the assessment. Chapter 4 will help you to assess your learning gaps and whether the challenges of what you need to learn to achieve your vision are manageable. Chapter 5 will look at other obstacles and constraints in the way of achieving your ambitions.

ENDNOTE

Trust your intuition in carrying out these and other exercises in this book. I remember once helping a scientist through career work. He worked diligently on each of my processes in a disciplined, logical way but yearned for some sort of score sheet or diagnosis to give him the right scientific answer for his particular personality and set of circumstances.

It just doesn't work like that. Use the exercises to provoke new insights then let your thoughts wander until they settle on some conclusions appropriate for you. The scientist came back to me two years later. One of the exercises had gnawed away at him until he was finally ready to listen to its message. Suddenly for him a cascade of conclusions tumbled out and he felt able to make a dramatic career switch that would never have come from a 'paint by numbers' approach.

Over the years I have been asked repeatedly which exercises are the most important. The answer is that it will be different for different people. Sometimes things which appear to me to be trivial or obvious turn out to be profoundly influential for the person I am working with — such as the time someone had not realised just how much they hated their job until they saw the mark on the far right of their lifeline exercise. This was the crucial trigger to convince them that they could not procrastinate about a career change any longer. Or the person inspired to turn his hobby into a job, despite the pay cut, when he felt the energy that he had put into that part of his mindmap. It had reminded him of a quotation he had heard attributed to motivational writer Dennis Wheatley: 'Follow your passions not your pension.' He had liked the quote, and agreed with it. But now he *believed* it.

CHAPTER 3

WHAT WOULD YOU REALLY LIKE TO DO?

Key ideas in this chapter:
- *Future of work*
- *Work versus Jobs*
- *Creating a Personal Vision*
- *Alternative Processes*
- *First Steps*

The last chapter got you to look at where you have been in your career to date. This chapter gets you to look forward. Some people get stuck on the question 'What would I really like to do?' so several alternative processes are presented. Choose which one or ones work best for you:

- ☑ You can create a Personal Vision and then work towards that.
- ☑ You can clarify a broad direction, then work in terms of 'more of this' and 'less of that'.

☑ You can identify a positive first step to get you moving, then create options from there once you have momentum.

Timescale is important. The British business guru Charles Handy (writer of *The Age of Unreason* and other books) suggests that people should work on a five-year horizon for their career planning. Other experts would agree. People change, life stages change, and equally importantly, occupations change.

It is thought that there is a 50 per cent chance that the occupation that today's 10-year-old will do when they grow up does not yet exist. Other occupations, or some of the skill sets they require, will become obsolete. If you need demonstration of the truth of this, just try to cast your mind back 10 or 15 years. How are organisations, technologies and jobs different between then and now? Now try to project 10 to 15 years forward.

So, five years is probably about right for career-planning purposes.

Occupations and skills are not the only things that are changing. The concepts of jobs, employment and workplaces are also constantly evolving, so it is worthwhile looking at some trends before going any further.

FUTURE WORK OPTIONS

In various contexts this book refers to 'work' and 'jobs'. But nowadays 'work' does not necessarily mean the same thing as 'workplace' and 'job' does not necessarily imply a relationship with a single 'employer'.

Here are some trends to start you thinking about how you may choose to work in the future. These are just a few thoughts from commentators about trends related to how people work:

What would you really like to do?

- In the mid to late 20th century more people found employment in services than in making things. Increasingly, that employment has shifted towards knowledge work – using experience, brainpower and creativity to access, interpret, adapt, reinvent and use information to offer something new or valuable. Jobs have progressively moved from agriculture to manufacturing to services to knowledge work.

- Larry Prusack, one-time head of Knowledge Management for IBM, talks about more Western jobs being in 'knowledge cousin' areas (e.g. design, consultancy, film-making etc) where the skill is in manipulating and applying scarce or specialist knowledge. Routine 'making thing' jobs will chase cheap labour costs to Asia and elsewhere.

- Typically, now over 80 per cent of the value of a company is in its intellectual capital rather than its tangible assets. That intellectual capital walks out of the door at the end of the day and goes home. Your employability rests on what you know and what you can do, rather than on the stability of the company for which you work.

- The structure of organisations is changing. Charles Handy compares the new emerging structure to a 'shamrock', the three-leaved plant. One leaf is the core – the small number of permanent staff with the central competencies that the company needs. This is supplemented by contractors and consultants (the second leaf) for skilled non-core work such as human resources or accounting. The third leaf represents temps and part-timers for routine jobs and for ebbs and flows of demand. The organisation only really invests in the development of the core people, the rest are hired as required, with the skills as required for the moment.

- Handy also says that you should find a customer not a job. Build a portfolio of your skills and experience. Work for several or serial employers to meet all your different needs. Self-employment and contracting will become even more prevalent than the one in five who do it today. Already the majority of workers do not work full time either, at least not for a single employer.

- The old unwritten contract of mutual loyalty between employer and employee (job security in exchange for loyal effort) has broken down, according to Michael Arthur, professor of management at Suffolk University (and author of *The Boundaryless Career*). Organisations restructure as required, and employees shift between employers as suits their own personal interest. The results are short, time-limited contracts, serial work, and self-directed career plans.

- Office blocks are used for about 50 hours out of 168 in the week. This is a grossly inefficient use of expensive resources. So, increasingly the nine-to-five and Monday-to-Friday office-based job will cease to be the norm, especially as technology enables other arrangements. People will work from home or car as their office. There will be a clear separation of work from workplace.

The conclusion is that you should think not only about what you want to do for your future work, but also how, where and for whom.

CREATING A PERSONAL VISION

What is a Personal Vision? It could be any of the following things, or all of them:

- ☑ A statement of your life's purpose.
- ☑ A description of how you want to live your life and spend your time and energies.
- ☑ A description of what you want to do.
- ☑ A description of a career destination or a continuing journey.

In essence, because it is personal, then it is whatever is going to be most useful to channel your energies. You want something that motivates you to move forward. You also want something that you can use when you get to a decision point or face a dilemma. It should help you to distinguish which options take you closer to what you want and which do not. It is more useful as a reference point than as a wall plaque.

The simplest process for creating a vision is just to sit down and think about the bullet points above (or whichever of them appeal to you), jot down your ideas and gradually work with them until a coherent vision emerges. It could take the form of a sentence, a set of bullet points, a picture or whatever else is meaningful to you.

If you need a more structured approach, try the following exercise. It is deceptively simple, but do not be tempted to rush it.

1. Go somewhere where you can feel relaxed and where you can think without interruption.

2. Spend five to ten minutes contemplating the 'result' of your

life. Think about yourself at an advanced age looking back over your life with feelings of total satisfaction. What is it that made you satisfied? You may 'hear' friends and family celebrating your life: what are they saying? Allow yourself to dream freely. Your thoughts may be about achievements, the work you did, the people you worked with, or your style of being — whatever is important to you.

3. Next, write down words or phrases which express important elements of this dream. Put down the first words that come into your head. Do not edit your thoughts at all.

4. Walk away from this list for a while. Let it 'incubate'.

5. When you come back to your list, examine each element for any self-imposed obstacles limiting your imagination or your choices (e.g. fears, practical considerations, doubts about your ability etc).

6. By now, you will be starting to get a feeling for what you really want and for what is less important to you. You may recognise some things that had previously seemed important but now seem less so.

7. Start to pull your ideas into a personal statement of your vision: 'These are the things I want from my career and my life.' Concentrate more on getting the core ideas right rather than the grammar.

8. Examine your draft to see if it covers any of the following which are important to you:
    self-image
    tangibles (e.g. money, material goods)

What would you really like to do?

    relationships
    home/health
    work and personal aspects
    community
    status/recognition
    other considerations

Your statement does not need to include all of the items, just those you particularly want to capture.

9. Expand and clarify your vision by asking yourself the following question about each of the things you want:'If I get this, what will it bring me?' The question should be repeated until you get to underlying, core values.

10. When you have your vision the way you want it, you will know it. You will get a 'Yes, this is right' feeling. At this stage, share it with people who are important to you. The more you talk about it the clearer it will become.

By way of an example, here is the personal vision for my career. Other people may express their vision in a different form (e.g., some may have dates, measures or specific numbers). But this works for me.

My vision:

☑ Develop and express my creativity/potential through my work/music/writing.

☑ Work and life in balance so that:
    — I work for pleasure, not for need;
    — I have enough time and quality of time for family/relationships;

- I can support the visions/goals of those I love;
- I stay healthy.

☑ Stretch my capabilities, not my endurance.

I couple this vision with some annual goals which I review each year. Producing this book is actually one of those goals. Another regular goal ensures that a proportion of my work each year is outside my comfort zone.

This vision-led approach has served me well. I refer to it when I need reminding about why I work or when I feel that I need a bit of a boost. I also use it as a reference when I have an important choice to make. For example, I once had to choose between an interesting but poorly paid project or a very lucrative dull one. It felt right to choose the interesting one.

At another time I had let my enthusiasm for my work (and the income it brought in) get out of hand. I had let my life get out of balance and the vision helped me to realise the correction needed. At that point I added a new bullet point for a time: not just earning more money, but earning more interesting money.

Of course, it is easy for vision statements to just become gimmicks or slogans, so you have to use them actively. I keep a copy of mine in the front of my diary and regularly ask myself whether I am true to it. It directs my career choices.

I created the personal vision for my career about eight years ago when I felt that I was putting more into my work than I was getting out of it. Over the years, the statement has helped me make a number of important choices and to keep a clearer sense of what I work for.

WHAT IF VISIONING DOES NOT WORK FOR YOU?

Not everyone responds to a vision. It may feel a bit too woolly or New Age for you. If that is the case, try this instead:

Make two lists:

- ☑ A list of all the important things that you want to have 'more of' in the future. Refer to your ideas from Chapters 2 and 3 for inspiration, but feel free to add extra items, including outside things that impact on your career (e.g. 'time with the family'; 'living in a better climate').
- ☑ A list of all the 'less of' items.

The 'more of' list is of greater importance because you want your career to move positively towards something rather than just helping you to escape from negative things. But the 'less of' list can also be important. It helps you to identify what you want to avoid or minimise in a job. And thinking about what you don't want sometimes gets you to think more about what you really do want too.

Spend a bit of time looking at your 'more of' list to isolate the priorities from the wish list items. One way to do this is to just go down the list marking each item either 'must have' or 'like to have'.

Another way to prioritise is to take 100 points and allocate them between the items on your list — the more important items should get most points and some items may get no points at all (which means they are effectively 'like to have' items rather than essentials). If you find yourself tempted to give equal points to lots of things, then force the decision by constraining your choices. Do this by using fixed multiples of points only: 20, 20, 10, 10, 10, 10, 5,

5, 5, 5. You can assign two multiples to an item (e.g. a 20 and a 5 to give 25 points), but you cannot split a 5-point block.

Your completed prioritised lists of 'more of' and 'less of' then become your reference point for future work choices. Each time you look at a new job option, you ask yourself whether it satisfies the needs in your lists better than your current work does. If it doesn't, then it is not a good move. If it does, are the gains enough to justify the jump?

WHAT IF YOU STILL CANNOT DECIDE WHAT YOU WANT?

As the saying goes: 'You don't drown by falling in the water, you drown by staying there.' Sometimes the longer that you are stuck in an unsatisfactory job, the harder it becomes to think of alternatives.

So it may be helpful just to get yourself moving to start with. Then once you have momentum, it may be easier to keep moving, but be more directed in your movement.

There are degrees of movement. Here are some ideas for areas where you could develop movement that helps towards progressing you forward with your career:

- ☑ Activities outside of worktime that would be positive: voluntary work, skill-building hobbies, study.
- ☑ Activities within the current job that might spark you into some new interests: projects, courses, work relationships.
- ☑ Shifts out of the job that might get you moving: a different job/occupation; a change to part-time work or contracting; enrolment in education.

The first items on the above list attract a lower level of risk than

What would you really like to do?

a complete job change does. Therefore, they may be a good place to start if you are reluctant to jump all the way.

Remember, once you start moving, it grows your confidence to take the next, bigger step.

SUMMARY

Having a Personal Vision helps you move forward by giving you something big and future-focused to aim for. There isn't a hard-and-fast formula; just include those elements which are important to you. The value of a vision is to direct your energies and actions towards a future goal.

Some people do not find a vision either easy to construct or useful. For them, a general direction and knowledge of the first steps is more valuable.

ENDNOTE

Some people construct a vision such as 'To be a millionaire by the age of 45' or 'Retire at 40'.

If that is what they really want, then there is nothing wrong with this. It identifies that financial accumulation is important to them and their focus should be on money-making activities (somewhere else they would need to identify how they will make that money). They would also need to be very clear about all the things that they would have to sacrifice on the journey (e.g. family time, discretionary spending, perhaps even 'fun' in the short term).

If they are not absolutely clear on all these pre-requisites, then it is not a vision, it is just a daydream.

But it may also be that their vision statement is not fully

accurate, and that financial accumulation is not really what they are looking for. A useful question to ask for these sorts of specific material ambitions is: 'If I got this, what would it give me?' The answer may be:

- It would give me the financial freedom to do what I like.
- It would give me wide options.
- People would see that I have been successful.
- I could travel around the world.

In these cases, the real vision may be more about 'freedom of choice,' 'status/recognition' or 'creating more leisure time' than becoming a millionaire for its own sake. If you are clear about the distinction between means and ends, then you can make better decisions about your career journey.

Chapter 4

UPGRADING YOUR SKILLS

Key ideas in this chapter:

Lifetime learning

Learning needs

Training versus non-training needs

Skills and Strengths

Permission to use a skill

Training options

Training plans

Finding the time

The process in this chapter is simple. First analyse your current and predicted learning needs. Then identify the smartest ways to meet those needs.

THE NEED FOR CONTINUOUS LIFETIME LEARNING

There is a simple lesson from biology: if a species changes faster than its environment does, then it survives. If it doesn't, it won't.

The same law applies to people. In the turbulent modern world this means that your learning and education cannot stop when you leave school or university, but must continue to be updated throughout life. Otherwise you face the organisational equivalent of extinction.

Traditionally, employers have organised and funded in-service training and development, investing in 'growing its own timber'. Greater job mobility, reduced loyalty and fluid structures mean that you cannot rely on this pattern any longer.

It is your career so take charge. Invest in yourself where you feel this is necessary. And negotiate with your employer for a contribution of time and money where there is a mutual benefit to be had.

IDENTIFYING LEARNING NEEDS

People don't know what they don't know. So if you organise your development plan by looking at brochures from course providers, you may be attracted to things that reinforce what you are already good at and ignore the things you really need to improve on.

There is a more systematic process you should take.

Look first for any 'skill gaps' in your current job. You can use a process very similar to the mindmap in Chapter 2, if this works for you. Mindmap the full range of skills needed in your current job (if mindmapping does not suit you, draw up a list).

Next, rate your skills against each heading. Use a three-point scale:

1 = inadequate
2 = meets the needs of the job
3 = strength beyond the needs of the job.

Look for objective evidence to support your ratings. For example,

Upgrading your skills

ask colleagues or examine your actual work output. You have nothing to gain by inflating your ability, nor by inappropriate modesty.

SEPARATING TRAINING AND NON-TRAINING NEEDS

An observation may have struck you as you did this exercise. There are some areas where you have the ability but your performance is lacking. Maybe you avoid those areas because you do not enjoy them or you make yourself too busy in other areas so you do not have time to do them.

This leads to a basic test of a training need: *could you do it if your job depended on it?* If you are genuinely unable to do it, then it represents a training need. But if you could do it (but don't do it) then it is not a training need, and training will not help you. You may need to examine your motivation or your work habits.

An example will make the distinction between training and non-training needs clear. I used to get into trouble at home for not doing the washing-up. Do you think I could have done it if my job (or my relationship) depended on it? Certainly. So sending me on a 'How to do washing up' course would not help. Nor would it motivate me. The discipline and motivation are things that I need to do for myself. I may do this by recognising the importance of the task in the bigger picture (in this case, maintaining a good relationship!); by creating a routine/discipline/habit; by creating little rewards for doing boring/unpleasant tasks; by goal-setting and so on. One way or another, if I need to perform and I am able to perform and if non-performance will hold me back, then I need to deal with it.

In conclusion, training will not solve non-training issues. So, with your skills list be clear which are the training issues and which are not, and deal with them separately.

The likelihood is that, for a number of your '1' ratings, you have the skill but you choose not to use it. Training won't cure that, but self-discipline will.

The remaining '1' ratings identify your current learning needs.

LOOKING AHEAD TO THE FUTURE

You can apply the same kind of approach to future jobs leading towards your vision, or for changes that you foresee in your current role. The process may need a little more input from others though, to specify what skills are needed. Fortunately, there is a simple way to obtain that information.

Start by identifying potential jobs or occupations that are consistent with your vision (Chapter 7 offers more help with this if you need it). Then look at your target job or occupation. If you know someone doing that role now, talk to them. If you cannot talk to them, observe them. But make your observations precise. You are only interested in two questions:

1. What do they do?

2. What is involved in doing that?

'What they do' identifies the skills that they employ. It is irrelevant what they enjoy, or find challenging. You need the *doing* words. 'What is involved' breaks down those skills to the next levels of detail to identify the skills more specifically.

So, for example, a person might 'lead the team'. What is involved in doing that? Perhaps they 'run team meetings', 'coordinate individual projects', 'manage conflicts and disagreements' and so on. Some of these items may require further levels of 'what is involved' observation to identify them more precisely.

The end point is a list of doing words – a skills list. Match yourself against this list using the same 3-point scale outlined above. You now have a list of your current skills and development needs and also the new skills that you want to acquire in the future. This will form a big part of creating your own training plan.

SKILLS AND PERMISSION

There is one additional consideration when looking at future skills. There may be some skills areas where you would rate yourself '2' or '3', but a prospective boss would rate you '1' because you were unproven or lacked experience. You are confident that you *have* the skill, you just need *permission* to use it.

In these cases, more training or qualifications will not solve the manager's concern, so identify these items separately. Here you need to *demonstrate* the skill in order to gain permission to use it. So your tactics need to concentrate on gathering compelling evidence of skill.

Here are some ideas:

- Look for areas in your work history where you have used those skills but they have not been visible to others. Can you highlight these areas?

- Look for opportunities within your job to negotiate small-scale demonstrations of these skills. Examples may include volunteering for projects, deputising, rotational duties and so on.

- Are there places outside work where you can demonstrate and use these skills then cite the evidence back to an employer? For example, there may be opportunities in community work, interest groups, hobbies etc to build and demonstrate the skills.

Investing time here may be as important to your career development as any training or education course can be. So plan for this possibility if you need it, in just the same way that you may plan for training and development needs.

Addressing your learning needs: your training options

Your list of '1' ratings may be very long. If it is too long, you may want to consider whether your vision is realistic or whether your timescale is too condensed. But assuming your list of learning needs is manageable, you can proceed to putting in place a training and development plan for yourself.

Winston Churchill once said 'I am always ready to learn, but I do not always like to be taught'. Fortunately, there are plenty of alternative ways to learn that do not involve going on training courses. So match your *needs* (the '1' items) to the *best options* for learning for you. This will keep your expenses on learning down, both in terms of time and money, and it will focus your efforts on the smartest learning tactics.

Here are some alternative learning tactics for you to consider. As you read down the list, think about the benefits and drawbacks of each in your own case.

- Internal training courses
- External training courses
- Full-time or part-time education
- Distance-learning education

Upgrading your skills

- ☑ Internet courses
- ☑ Buying or borrowing books
- ☑ On-the-job coaching by your manager
- ☑ On-the-job coaching by others
- ☑ Finding yourself a mentor
- ☑ Structured observation or buddying opportunities with experts
- ☑ Visits to other sites/businesses
- ☑ Project team involvement
- ☑ Involvement in higher-level managerial thinking/decision-making
- ☑ Expanding your duties/responsibilities
- ☑ Negotiating for more delegated tasks
- ☑ Deputising for others
- ☑ Special projects

PUTTING YOUR TRAINING PLAN TOGETHER

By this stage you should have a series of lists in front of you.

One list covers learning needs and identifies skills that you need to acquire or improve. Matched against these skills are the tactics that you will use to acquire the skills.

A second list may identify skills that you already have but which you need to discipline yourself to use so that your demonstrated performance matches your capability.

A third list may identify those areas where you need to accumulate

Changing Careers

experience or evidence of experience so that you can convince people to let you use the skills you have.

You cannot work on everything at once, but you may start to notice a number of areas where you can deal with several needs through one action. The main task now, though, is to prioritise your needs and solutions. Go through your lists again and make a plan of the order in which you need to address the identified items, scheduled over whatever timeframe you think is workable.

Finally, identify which of the areas you need to fully invest in yourself and in which areas you would seek help from your employer. Work out 'what is in it for them' for the employer areas, then you are ready to negotiate.

And if your employer is unwilling to commit resources to you, take charge yourself. Remember, it is *your* career.

SUMMARY

This chapter describes a systematic way in which to put together development plans for yourself. Firstly you identify skills gaps in your current role, then explore and add in skills that you believe you will need in your career future.

Then you separate out the training from the non-training issues and deal with those differently. For your training needs, you consider an array of learning methods so that you are not over-reliant on training courses or educational qualifications and so that you can better match the method to the skill need.

Finally you prioritise your needs and establish a realistic timeframe. You also decide which parts of the plan you need to commit to and which parts you would seek help with from your employer.

Upgrading your skills

ENDNOTE: MAKING THE TIME

Look at Diagram 5 below. This shows a 168-hour 'pie' — the fixed number of hours in a week. The segments marked on that pie indicate a typical pattern of time use:

- about 56 hours a week sleeping;
- about 30 hours on maintenance tasks eating, showering, dressing, toileting etc.);
- about 40 hours on work;
- the remaining 40 or 50 hours split between family, friends and interests, depending on personal circumstance.

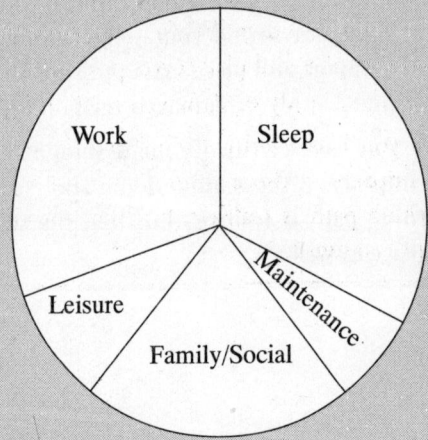

Diagram 5: How you spend the 168 hours in a week

Here's the question: What happens if you want to start investing, say 10 hours a week, on developing new skills for your career development? (For example, through registering for a tertiary education course.) Which slice does the 10 hours come out of?

Probably, it does not come out of sleep or maintenance time. Unless you have negotiated with your employer, it will not come out of work time either (and even where you have negotiated, they will probably expect you to meet them halfway, so you will still have five hours to find).

The reality is that the time is most likely to come from the areas of least resistance, which probably means family, social and leisure time. If you know this and have specifically discussed this with your family, they are more likely to support you.

If it was not discussed, they will just notice your absence or a perceived unwillingness to pull 'your weight around the house.' This will erode support and place extra pressure on you. It may end in discontinued study or damaged relationships.

So, once you have clarified your development plan, talk through the impacts on those around you and ensure not only that the learning path is realistic, but that the support structures are in place as well.

Chapter 5

DEALING WITH OBSTACLES AND CONSTRAINTS

Key ideas in this chapter:

Anxieties

Types of Obstacles

Fixed Constraints

Tactics to Handle Obstacles

Substitute Factors

Potential Losses in Career Changes

Managing Risk

'Obstacles are what you see when you take your eye off the goal.'
(anon.)

If you own a house, you probably have a mortgage. Your job helps service that mortgage. But it is unlikely that the purpose of your career is to repay the bank. The mortgage is just one example of a career obstacle. Obstacles need to be factored into your career plan, but they should not dominate it.

Changing Careers

This chapter focuses on the obstacles in the way of making your career change. The aim is to devise tactics for dealing with short-term or moveable obstacles and to find ways of accommodating those things you cannot change. Realism needs to inform your career plan, but the crucial point is that your *vision* should drive your career, not your *obstacles*.

TURNING ANXIETIES INTO PROBLEMS

The little voice in your head that has said, 'Yes but ...' to you throughout this book so far may be hard to keep quiet. It is not very helpful. It just stops you from acting. But just telling it to go away does not solve the problem; it has a serious message that you need to attend to. The trouble is that while those messages are expressed as vague anxieties, they are hard to deal with. So first explore them and convert them into specific problems. Then it will be easier to decide what to do with each concern.

Types of Obstacles

Here are some generic headings of areas in which you might face obstacles or limitations on your free choices:

- *Personal physical* – factors such as disabilities; age or youth; health issues; physical ability, strength or coordination; appearance relative to 'norms' (whatever they are!)

- *Personal psychological* – lack of confidence; shyness; risk aversion or other internal factors

- *Personal historical* – sensitivity about past record (e.g. prison, past failings, or job dismissal); narrow or limited work history; time out of the workforce

Dealing with obstacles and constraints

- *Geographical* – where you choose to live relative to where the jobs or markets are; infrastructure (e.g. commuting ease, Internet access, access to state funds, tax issues, local laws etc)

- *Educational* – level of qualifications; age or type of qualification; fluency in language; base skills such as driving, writing or computing; poor study skills or confidence discouraging you from future study

- *Financial obligations* – mortgage and other outgoings; lack of reserves (e.g. money 'for a rainy day' or retirement savings); current debts; spending habits; future spending plans and ambitions; lack of start-up capital

- *Family and social* – dependants (e.g. children or parents: cost and time); status as sole breadwinner; commitments to church, iwi or other groups; need for your plans to fit in with the plans of others (e.g. partner's career or children's schooling); degree of family/social support available to you; perceived prejudice based on your gender, sexuality, ethnicity etc

- *Values* – concepts of what you will or will not do or where you will or will not work; life/work balance considerations; future personal plans (e.g. to have a family, travel etc).

Your first task is to use this list as a starting point for identifying your own personal obstacles. You may think of other things which are not on this list. Add them in. It is your private list so put everything down on it that concerns you.

Once your list is complete, you can start to analyse it by asking:

- ☑ Which concerns are 'real' and which are created by your own imagination?
- ☑ Which are fixed and immoveable and which represent choices that you could un-choose?
- ☑ Which are temporary or short term and which are permanent?

Immediately some items will begin to drop off as being 'silly' concerns or things that you could overcome if you put your mind to it. Others may point to a specific remedy (e.g. 'complete my degree'; 'put aside $100 per week to build an emergency fund'). Others may be resolvable by talking them through or negotiating them with the people concerned.

Yet others may be real but may only affect the timing of your career plan (e.g. 'wait until the children leave school' or 'get the mortgage down further'). Before you delay, though, ask yourself if there are other things you could be using this time for that may ultimately advance your goal. For example, could you acquire relevant qualifications or experience or establish useful networks in the mean time?

The obstacle then becomes a *feature* on the path of your plan rather than a *setback* to its achievement.

Fixed Constraints

The list of obstacles should be getting shorter. But there might still be some big items to consider. One or two may be immoveable in your life (e.g. a serious health issue or a fixed decision not to move home). If these obstacles are truly incompatible with your career goal, then the goal may be unrealistic and need to be modified.

Dealing with obstacles and constraints

Some, however, may make the goal more difficult, but not impossible. For example, would a disability *prevent* you from doing the job or would it *condition* how you go about doing it? If the issue is 'how', focus your attention on this aspect of the problem.

The disability example illustrates another point. The disability may not affect your ability to *do* the job but it may influence your ability to *win* the job. If this is the case, consider how you could go about demonstrating your ability to the prospective employer to overcome their preconceptions about you.

Tactics to handle Obstacles

The key tactic is to focus on the issue to establish the real, underlying problem, so that the solutions become more apparent.

This approach can be applied to many obstacles — money, for example. If achieving your goal requires more money than you have access to, then ask:

- How could I launch the idea without money?
- Could I drip-feed money in as it became available — perhaps by scaling back my ambition over a longer timeframe?
- Could I get others to put money in (as a loan, a joint venture, a franchise)?

An example that comes to mind is that of the woman who craved to become a self-employed training consultant. Unfortunately, she lacked trainer skills, business skills and a client base. As sole breadwinner for her family, she feared they would all starve if she made the leap from the job she hated to follow her dream. But she worked out her tactics.

First, she joined the local training association and attended their

Changing Careers

monthly meetings to build a network. She then used some of her annual leave to assist a trainer consultant friend with a couple of courses. She did this for free, but in exchange acquired some coaching on business aspects of the role and some of the classroom trainer skills.

Next, she designed a series of classes for one of the local evening colleges. She got her friend to critique it, then approached the college. Colleges don't pay well, but it covered her childcare and helped her build further experience. She took this experience back to her employer who then gave her a training project associated with her normal job, but stretching her a bit.

Within six months she had a set of embryonic skills, plus ample demonstration of her commitment. The training consultant offered her a job as a junior trainer, which then became senior trainer, then involvement as a partner and co-owner. The whole process took four or five years, but by following a plan she got there.

A different example concerns the man whose absolute terror of flying had disqualified him in the eyes of his bosses from consideration for management positions where travel was deemed essential. He recognised this phobia as a real and immovable constraint. So he looked around to identify other large organisations which tended to be less geographically spread. He then went to work in a local authority where his progress would be determined by his skills and achievements, not his weaknesses.

SUBSTITUTE FACTORS

Sometimes it is worth thinking about the things that you can substitute which would be of equivalent value for your purpose. A couple of examples may illustrate this.

The first picks up directly from the money-shortage case above.

Dealing with obstacles and constraints

If you have no money, could you substitute another resource — 'sweat equity' for example? 'Sweat equity' is where you put in the labour and someone else puts up capital. The dollar value of your time represents your stake or the proportion of your ownership in the venture, agreed at the outset.

Another form of substitution takes you back to an earlier idea: transferable skills. If specific obstacles prevent you from achieving a goal, could you take your skills and apply them equally elsewhere to the same benefit?

Say you wanted to set up a small horticultural venture, but your location was fixed and the climate was wrong for your chosen crop — could you grow something else? Chances are that you would use the same or similar skills to do this.

Similarly, if you yearned for a strategic role but all the corporate offices had shifted offshore, could you substitute 'public sector', 'not-for-profit' or 'small business' into your vision?

POTENTIAL LOSSES IN CAREER CHANGES

Change is not uniformly positive. There is always something to lose as well as something to gain in any transition. What have you got to lose?

For a person contemplating a mid-career shift, there is potentially a lot more to lose than for someone at the start of a career. Partly this is explainable by outside commitments which go with the mid-career life-stage: family responsibilities, mortgages, retirement appearing over the horizon and so on.

But partly the perceived losses arise from your success to date. You have a lot invested in your current career, skills and experience. If you were to move into another field, the chances are that some of these accumulated intellectual assets would become redundant.

Changing Careers

The bigger the change, the more you risk losing. Similarly, you may lose some of the trappings of your current success: status, recognition, seniority, remuneration level and so on. If you moved into a new field, you would possibly have to start at a more junior level than the one you currently enjoy.

Just as with the potential obstacles above, list your potential losses. Which would be real? Which would be temporary or short term? Which would be definite as opposed to possible losses?

Which potential losses would really matter to you? Do these represent things that matter *more* than your need for career change? If so, stay where you are and accept the consequences.

However, if they matter for now, but you can foresee a time when they will matter less, change the *timing* of your plan. And if they matter in the long term and you want to avoid the loss, can you find a way of carrying what is important with you into your future work?

Assessing Risk

Some of the concerns you have identified in this chapter may be about things that are not actual and definite, but about things that *may* happen in the future. You *may* face financial setbacks; your health *may* deteriorate; you *may* lose earning power; you *may* lose the ability to use certain skills; your new career *may* not work for you.

Imagination can turn maybes into disaster scenarios. So it is worth rounding off this chapter with some ideas from the field of risk management.

First think about the potential *impact* if a specific problem did eventuate. Use a 10-point scale if you like (10 = 'end of the world'; 1 = 'minor inconvenience').

Dealing with obstacles and constraints

Next think about the *likelihood* of that occurrence (10 = 'certain to happen'; 1 = 'extremely unlikely').

Then you can combine these two scores to indicate the real level of risk (giving yourself a score out of a hundred).

$$\text{Risk} = \text{Impact} \times \text{Likelihood}$$

This formula helps to put your risks into perspective.

For example, an event like a major earthquake may have devastating consequences, but if the likelihood is very low, then you would not organise your entire life around earthquake-avoidance. You might, however, choose to make sensible preparations.

So a score of 100 would be a very serious risk, and one you would be foolish to ignore. A '30' risk would be more serious than a '20'. But maybe you could lower the overall risk by reducing the score in one of the factors using some risk management tactics.

For those risks that you thought were significant enough to respond to, there are some common tactics to consider:

- ☑ Could you minimise the likelihood of occurrence?

- ☑ Could you reduce or prevent the impact if it happened?

- ☑ Could you repair the damage quickly if it happened – through planning or insurance etc?

You can apply these risk considerations to career thinking in several ways. Firstly, you can avoid blowing potential losses or problems out of all perspective to create disaster movies in your head! Secondly, you can tackle your concerns in terms of tactics to minimise the downside risks that go with change.

A colleague who wanted to move into self-employment as

a consultant feared that he would have a six- to nine-month period with no income while he built up a client base. The 'impact' would have been catastrophic (losing his house). But he was able to minimise the 'likelihood' factor by arranging a short-term part-time contract back with his old employer to provide enough income to cover his household expenses while he went about building market presence for himself. This brought down his overall risk exposure.

A second colleague wanted a business for himself and his family; something they could build together and where they could keep the rewards of their efforts. He feared that their business acumen was not strong enough, though, and that they would lose their life savings. They decided to lower the risk by buying into a franchise outlet where the franchise company provided systems and training in exchange for fees. The profits would be lower, but the likelihood of them falling over was minimised and the impact was limited to the amount of money they had invested. Later, they intended to quit the franchise and set up their own venture, but this tactic lowered the risk in the meantime.

SUMMARY

Obstacles are easier to address if they are acknowledged and if they are made specific. So the first task is to list your obstacles, then to analyse them.

If an obstacle is big, real and immoveable, then you may need to change your goal. On the other hand, you may just need to change the plan — the timing or tactics — for achieving your goal.

Many other obstacles are either temporary (in which case you adjust your timing), imagined (in which case you put them into perspective), or choices that you can change (negotiate, or decide, what is really important to you).

Dealing with obstacles and constraints

With mid-career shifts, there are always losses as well as gains. Identifying those losses can help you minimise them or accept them.

Career thinking needs to be realistic. But you have a choice between surrendering to reality or deciding how you choose to manage it.

ENDNOTE

Stephen Covey (author of Seven Habits of Highly Effective People) used to ask people to think about the situations in which they had failed to enact their plans. He asked them whether they felt the problem was:

- that they could not *prioritise* what they really wanted, or
- that they could not *organise* themselves to implement their plans, or
- that they lacked *self-discipline* to carry out their plans.

Most people identified the third factor as their shortcoming. Covey disagreed. In this view, the first factor was most likely the problem in most cases: if you want something enough, then you will move heaven and earth to get it. But some people write lists of 'goals' or 'priorities', but don't really commit to them fully.

For instance, the Viking invaders used to burn their boats, so that there was no turning back. This guaranteed they would put their total effort into moving forward — they were committed.

Thus, transition tactics (such as the contract with an ex-employer described above) are okay to help manage obstacles or risks, but be wary of hedging your bets too much. If you do things half-heartedly you are more likely to fail. Re-examine your vision. What do you *really* want?

CHAPTER 6

PULLING IT TOGETHER: CREATING THE PLAN

Key ideas in this chapter:

List of Tasks

Timetabling

Short-term Actions and First Steps

Plan B

Keeping Motivation

Knowing-Doing Gap

This chapter could have been positioned after Chapter 7 – Job Seeking – but the logic here is that you should not narrow your focus down to a particular job application until you have a clear career plan.

However, you cannot finalise your career plan until you know what job(s) you are aiming at. So, read about the principles in this chapter, then read ahead, then finalise your plan.

This chapter lists the planning tasks for you, then invites you to create a realistic schedule for completing those tasks. It is not

Pulling it together: creating the plan

sufficient just to have a five-year vision; unless you are doing something now towards realising that vision, it will perpetually remain five years away from you.

THE PLANNING TASKS

Here is a list of key tasks to perform (including tasks already covered in this book and some not yet covered). You may have been working on some already, and you may have other tasks of your own to add to the list. The list is laid out in approximate order, but some tasks may need to shift position for you. Recognise also that many tasks can occur at the same time:

1. Do the exercises in this book about your past/present.
2. Work out your total skills and your preferred skills (see Chapter 2, especially pages 30ff).
3. Create your personal vision (see Chapter 3, especially page 41).
4. List your key values and other key elements of your preferred work (see Chapter 2, especially pages 27 and 28).
5. Identify those skills you want to develop strengths in (see Chapter 4, page 52).
6. Research the categories of ideal jobs (see Chapter 7, page 83).
7. Identify skills gaps: those skills you need to improve on in order to meet the job requirements (see Chapter 7, page 83 and Chapter 4, page 52).
8. Identify obstacles in the way of your career choice (see Chapter 5).

Changing Careers

9. Identify constraints on your career choice (see Chapters 3, 4 and 5).

10. Devise tactics for dealing with each of the obstacles and constraints (see Chapter 5).

11. Research your training and development options and create a plan (see Chapter 4).

12. Implement your training plan (see Chapter 4 and this chapter).

13. Create your self-marketing plan (see Chapter 7).

14. Initiate networking and other marketing tactics (see Chapter 7).

15. Identify and secure any interim jobs/experience opportunities you need (see Chapters 5 and 7).

16. Identify specific jobs you want, consistent with your vision etc (see Chapter 3 for vision and Chapter 7 for jobs).

17. Devise specific tactics to secure that job (see Chapter 7).

18. Take up your ideal job.

19. Update your career plan – do this regularly.

TIMETABLING THE TASKS

The example on pages 74–75 shows what a timetable might look like. The person in the example sought to move from a stressful front-line operational health worker role into a strategic public policy role, not necessarily in the health sector. She had already worked out her vision, although she was open to the likelihood of this evolving as she implemented the steps of her plan.

Pulling it together: creating the plan

In the actual case above, the plan did change. Internships were hard to find and employers wanted people with policy experience as well as policy qualifications. So she accepted a policy-related job as a stepping stone. This opened up different avenues for her development and the vision changed again. (Once more, this example reinforces the point that moving forward is more important than getting the plans 100 per cent right.)

For your first draft of a timetable, carry out two exercises:

1. Start at the end (say, five years from now) and work back to today;
2. Start with today and work forward to your vision.

Put all the tasks into your timetable and assign 'guestimated' start and finish dates to each one.

The first exercise helps you crystallise your realism and your sense of urgency. Consider the following example to see how this may be so.

Suppose your vision requires you to retrain by completing a tertiary qualification. If your end point is an ideal job in five years, then working backwards to today tells you how soon you would need to start studying. That may provoke the following options:

- ☑ studying several papers each year, starting now;
- ☑ enrolling full-time in the next year or so (is that feasible?);
- ☑ pushing out the end date for securing your ideal job.

Changing Careers

	This month	*Within three months*
1. Identify suitable postgraduate course	Get brochures from universities	Select course and enrol
2. Work out a budget for study	Talk to husband re course fees and break in earnings	Build up a reserve fund of cash; implement tighter home budget
3. Study		
4. Time management issues		
5. Identify suitable job		Talk to variety of people about policy jobs content and availability

Pulling it together: creating the plan

Within six months	Within 12 months	One year or later
	Start course	Finish course after two years
Resign from current job	Take up course	Finish course
Talk to husband about reallocating domestic tasks to make time for study		
	Choose course unit options and projects that will expose her to two to three likely sectors; decide which sector appeals most	Upgrade CV; brush up on interviewing skills; explore internship options; apply for jobs

The 'start with today and plan forward' approach enables you to think about what practical actions you can fit into your busy life. Here are some headings for the timescale:

- ☑ this week
- ☑ this month
- ☑ next three months
- ☑ next three months after that
- ☑ next six months after that
- ☑ next year after that
- ☑ next year after that etc.

Of course, you can put in actual calendar dates. The key points are that the start is *immediate*, the short-term timeframe is *specific* and the whole plan is *itemised*.

The previous section listed 19 planning steps. Identify the ones which apply to you and the specific tasks that you need to do for each. Then place them into your timetable where you think that they fit. Work through to the logical completion of the plan.

If the end turns out to be 15 years from today, then you know that you either need to:

- ☑ scale down your ambition
- ☑ accept a longer timeframe, or
- ☑ get a move on; schedule more tasks sooner.

Institutions such as universities have cut-off dates for applications, enrolments and courses, so you may have to take these into account also.

Pulling it together: creating the plan

The danger of a five-year vision is that five years makes it seem like there is a lot of time, so why not start tomorrow or next week instead of today? Of course you already know the answer to that: if you are delaying starting, then you just keep pushing the end point ahead of you. The discipline of planning a timetable, particularly the short-term timetable, urges you into immediate action.

Cycle between the two methods until you have a realistic timetable for yourself and your situation. Document this as a table of tasks and times so that your ideas don't get lost or forgotten.

Then use the document to make sure that you do not drift from your plan. As you move forward, tick things off as you achieve them. And keep updating your plan so that there is always something specific in the 'this week' and 'this month' columns.

Recognise also that the plan may change. A plan does not need to be *right*. It just needs to be *useful*. It is quite possible that partway through your journey you will decide you want another destination. Fine. Just replan.

SHORT-TERM ACTIONS AND FIRST STEPS

Even if your vision is crystal clear, you know that without action it's just a daydream. So your plan should have identified some very clear first steps. Commit to these now. Get under way quickly to achieve forward momentum.

But pace yourself. You don't want to start with a hiss and a roar then run out of energy. If you have a steady stream of regular but small tasks, they are more likely to happen. Break the bigger tasks into small chunks with something to accomplish now and something later.

For some people (including the woman in the timetable example) the long-term vision is not totally clear or convincing, but the first steps are really obvious. This is okay. Use the power of short-term clarity to start you moving forward.

Remember, it is a lot easier to keep moving once you are in motion.

Have a Plan B

There is some truth in the old saying: 'A plan is a method of reaching the wrong destination with confidence.' Don't be afraid to let go of the plan if your goal shifts or the world changes. And if new obstacles arise, change tactics to navigate around them.

Inevitably at some point you will find that some part of your plan does not work. So create a Plan B. This means making some of your decisions flexible enough that you have some other options at key points. For example: if the course or the job is unavailable, what else could you do at that time?

Keeping yourself Motivated

As with any long-term project, sustaining motivation is both important and challenging. At the outset use this book and the strength of your desire for change to get you started. Once you are moving it is easy to maintain momentum.

Put some *key milestone* points in your timetable. These are points where you can say to yourself that you have completed a key task. Reward yourself in some small way. Share the experience with someone close to you.

Flick ahead to Chapter 8 and look at the table there (pages 96 and 97). This identifies some key motivating forces for change:

- ☑ strength of your vision
- ☑ knowledge of first steps

Pulling it together: creating the plan

- ☑ strength of your dissatisfaction with the status quo
- ☑ support resources
- ☑ advantages of changing.

Each of these motivating forces can be used to help you and the more clear each factor is in your mind, the more helpful it will be.

In an ideal world, you would be able to draw on all of them. In practice it may be that your vision is a bit fuzzy, say. But if your dissatisfaction is intense and you have some compelling first steps in mind, these factors can drive you to action. Similarly, if you have a really clear long-term vision and good support but you are unsure about the first steps, then you may want to just jump in and experiment. Try a lot of things and keep what works.

The more that you can build up each of these motivating forces, the more their additive power will help you.

The danger time for most projects is in the middle stages. This is when the newness and excitement of the project has worn off but before the end is in sight. So, set mini-projects for yourself and increase your rewards on their completion.

And most of all, keep moving forward.

SUMMARY

This chapter lists key planning tasks and invites you to create personalised timeframes and plans. Without a plan, your vision becomes just wishful thinking.

The importance of a steady flow of short-term tasks is to prevent the long-term goal staying forever in the long term. It is important to build in milestones and rewards to keep your motivation levels up. You may also want to refer back to the pie chart of time at the end of Chapter 4. Recognise that any extra time that you spend on your career work needs to come from some other time use (usually family, friends or leisure time), so be prepared to discuss and negotiate your plan with those around you.

ENDNOTE

Pfeffer and Sutton wrote a book called *The Knowing-Doing Gap* about how people don't always do the things they know they should. Some of the barriers to doing are relevant here:

- *Planning* substitutes for doing. Just because you have written a plan, doesn't mean it will happen. You also need to take action on your plan.
- *Thinking* substitutes for doing. Just because you have thought about it doesn't mean it will happen.
- *Talking/deciding* substitutes for action.

You get the point.

Chapter 7

JOB SEEKING

Key ideas in this chapter:
Where are the jobs?
Job Content
Marketing Yourself
Networking and Visibility
CVs and Interviews
Self-Employment
Managing Stress

The third of the three circles in Diagram 2 from Chapter 1 focused on 'what the job needs'. This is the last piece of the plan to put in place. This chapter will examine where the jobs are and how to gain access to them.

It will also briefly cover how to position yourself to be the best candidate for your chosen job. There are plenty of books around dealing with how to write winning CVs or how to succeed at interviews, so this ground will be covered only lightly.

The field of self-employment will also be looked at. There is no job application form or interview to determine whether you qualify for self-employment, so nobody is likely to tell you if you are wasting your time or start-up capital. They will just let you go bust. So, this chapter will also help you assess your suitability and preparedness for possible self-employment.

WHERE ARE THE JOBS?

Supposedly less than 30 per cent of job vacancies are advertised these days, with many of these circulated via organisation or agency websites rather than the traditional newspaper columns.

Furthermore, most job growth does not originate in large established companies, but emerges from small, growing companies. Often, these companies build jobs around 'the right people' when they find them, rather than having vacant slots waiting to be filled.

And an increasing number of companies employ contractors, consultants and temporary staff to meet non-core business needs. They hire and dispose of skills as they need them, expecting the owners of those skills to keep themselves up to date with current techniques and practice.

So, your radar for employment opportunities needs to be set wide to scan the full range of sources and it needs to be finely attuned to quickly identify opportunities when they come on screen.

JOB CONTENT NOT JOB TITLE

You want to find work which matches your vision, values and preferred skills. So, when you scan for jobs, look at job *content*, not job *title*. Bear in mind also that what you seek may not be contained in a single existing job. You may want to invent your own job or combine a 'portfolio' of jobs.

Job seeking

You may already know the job you want. If you do not, try the process below. It takes a bit of time, but it can be a worthwhile way of expanding your horizons (if they need expanding).

1. Brainstorm a list of jobs which you think may be interesting to you.

2. Think about people you know who actually work in those types of jobs. Don't rely on job adverts or job descriptions. They seldom give a full picture of the skills needed in a job.

3. Talk to a range of jobholders about what they do. Don't ask them whether they enjoy it or not. Your preferences and motivations are different from theirs, so that information is irrelevant. Focus on the full job and not just the glamorous bits.

4. Compare the list of what they do to your list of preferred skills you want to use. The greater the match between lists, the more likely that the job will suit you.

5. Move from person to person, job to job until you get nearer to identifying your goal. Your journey through different contacts may lead you into consideration of jobs that you had not thought about before. Yet you may find that there are some good matches with your transferable skills in unlikely places. This can lead to exciting new options.

6. You will know the right job when you see it.

You will also start to get a feeling for how long it will take you to get there, starting from where you are now. This is because you have matched the skills needed against the skills you have in your repertoire, so you have a clear view of the gaps.

You also have the core information for a very strong pitch to sell yourself to potential employers. You can tell them what skills you have that they need, and you can also propose tactics for addressing any deficiencies.

Once you have a specific role in mind, then consider approaching an employer with a proposal, whether they have an identified vacancy or not. This may be just the prod they need.

But make sure that your approach is well planned, with a specific proposal or role to present, evidence of your fit with that role, plus the benefits to the employer. Make it easy for them to say 'yes'. If the risks are high for them, think about ways that you could trial, demonstrate or pilot the suggested arrangement.

Marketing Yourself

'Marketing is what makes selling unnecessary' is an old but apt adage.

If you can do other things that avoid you having to 'door-knock' then that has got to be good news. Especially if those other things are more effective anyway.

Your three marketing tasks are, in sequence:

1. Make people aware of you and your skills;

2. Generate interest in you and your skills;

3. Get an employer to act on that interest by trying or buying what you have to offer.

Networking and Visibility

1. The first challenge is *awareness-building*, which means getting the right people to know about you. If they don't know about you, it is irrelevant how good you are.

Job seeking

If you are changing careers, people may already know you, but may have pigeonholed you into your old role. You may need to alter their awareness about you by presenting them with new evidence. Perhaps even by surprising them into reforming their preconceptions.

Instead of sending out 100 copies of your new CV (effectively, 'junk mail'), there are better ways to increase your visibility and at the same time display your credibility:

- ☑ network with people in your chosen field;
- ☑ run workshops or seminars on topics that will interest relevant people;
- ☑ serve on project or voluntary groups, using the skills you want people to see;
- ☑ join industry associations or lobby groups – but don't just join, participate;
- ☑ write articles – if you have expertise that a professional journal or a business publication may value, offer them a contribution. Some of the trade papers and local free newspapers look for newsworthy or interesting copy. Websites and 'blogs' offer another avenue. But don't expect to be paid. This is about exposure, not income.

These are all 'broadcast' tactics designed to expose you to a wider audience. So if you know specific individuals that you need to influence, you also need to hone in on them. They may be people that you have met via the networking and so on you have done above. Or they may be other people that you know or know of.

2. The next stage is generating interest. Your visibility tactics may do that for you, but still you probably need to approach key people offering useful information or some other proposed benefit. Seek a few minutes to present them with a proposition, a sales pitch if you like. This is what you offer; this is the benefit to them. Show them work samples if you can.

   Be proactive. Don't wait for them to offer you an interview. That just places you in the queue with all the others they choose to see at the same time.

3. Lastly, you need to make it easy for them to make you an offer. You could propose the offer yourself. Alternatively you could suggest a more reversible, and therefore less risky, approach such as a trial project, a short-term contract, or you could work free to demonstrate your worth and eagerness. Other alternatives include apprenticeship or joint venture. Use your imagination.

Of course many jobs are still filled via the traditional approach of curriculum vitae and interview. That is covered next.

THE ROLE OF THE CV

Your CV does not win you a job, it is merely your brochure. It may get you in the door for an interview or it may be the 'leave behind' material so they don't forget you. It needs to be informative and it needs to stand out. And it also needs to be tailored to the specific target. Review and revise your CV for each specific person or organisation you target. Demonstrate to the reader what you know about their needs and how you match those needs.

There are books (and agencies) that specialise in CV writing. Styles change from time to time, but the core elements that need to be included remain largely the same:

- ☑ how the employer can contact you;
- ☑ what your qualifications are, how current these are and how you keep up to date;
- ☑ what your work background is, the logic of your moves and the explanation of any gaps;
- ☑ your skills and strengths and the evidence to support any claims you make;
- ☑ a sense of you as a person, as conveyed by your interests and passions and how you present yourself.

Ultimately the reader wants to know what makes you special; why should they bother meeting you? If you have tailored your CV to their organisation and the job they offer, then there is likely to be something in there to stimulate their interest.

There are two additional considerations for a mid-career shifter to take into account:

1. Suppose you are contemplating a move to a new field. The new role may, of necessity, be of lower seniority and/or of lower pay than your old one. If you fudge the issue, then you leave yourself open to unhelpful assumptions that a prospective employer may make, such as 'We probably cannot afford this person' or 'If they are applying for a more junior job, would they be unhappy, or coasting or poorly motivated?' etc. Both are reasons to say no to you, without even investigating whether their assumptions are correct or not.

   You are better to front the issue directly. Tell them why you are changing careers and what your realistic expectations are.

2. The second, perhaps related issue is age. You may be older than

other potential candidates because you have had a prior career. With age discrimination illegal in many countries nowadays, you have the choice of leaving your date of birth off your CV.

But any recruiter with a mind to it could deduce your approximate age from your qualifications and job history. And they could always find a plausible legal excuse for rejecting you, if that was their inclination.

So again, why not front the issue by highlighting the compensating benefits that you offer that may offset any prejudice about age. Highlight experience, maturity, relationship skills etc. And if you suspect preconceived notions about say, energy levels or openness to new learning, surprise them with the evidence that dispels such myths in your case.

A FEW WORDS ABOUT THE INTERVIEW

Again there are numerous books out there on this topic. But an interview is no more than a two-way discussion in which the purpose is to exchange information. You probably do that every day without even being aware of it.

Do your research before the interview. Read the company reports. Check their website. Talk to informed people you may know.

Then make sure you tell the interviewer the things about you that you need them to know. Answer their questions, and provide the information and evidence that confirms that you have the skills, knowledge and attitude that the job requires.

What about your weaknesses or disadvantages?

If you assume there are typically eight people interviewed for one job, and that five of those people could do the job, then you can see that interviewing is in effect a process of elimination. Therefore,

Job seeking

to a degree at least, the interviewer is looking for evidence of why they should not offer you the job.

You could try to hide your flaws and limitations. Or you could show that you have thought about your limitations, and demonstrate how you would manage these so that they should not be of real concern. Then turn the focus onto the unique strengths that you would bring to the situation. The first points lessen the risk for the employer (and give them less reason to reject you), the latter give you a reason to stand out.

Finally, remember that an interview is a two-way exchange. You are also looking to make a decision, so ask questions and check out concerns. Make them want to impress you too.

SELF-EMPLOYMENT — THE OTHER OPTION

Up to 20 per cent of workers are now self-employed, some with 'regular' jobs at the same time. Anyone can choose self-employment, so if you prove unsuited to it then your first indication of this may be when you discover that your investment of time and money is unrecoverable.

Before trying out self-employment, you will probably think to assess your technical competencies as you would for a regular, employed job. But you should also look at whether you would be temperamentally suited to self-employment; whether you could handle it, and whether you would enjoy the demands.

Look first at your motivation to be self-employed:

1. *Being your own boss*

Freedom to decide, to implement your ideas and to escape bureaucratic management practices or a dead-end job — it sounds wonderful. But consider two 'reality' questions:

a) As your own boss, would you be a good boss? Would you push yourself hard enough, or too hard? Would you force yourself to confront weaknesses or blind spots?

b) How much real freedom would your chosen business allow you? You may end up reliant on a dominant customer or your bank/lender. Make sure realism informs your thinking.

2. Reward for effort

Frequently the extra reward comes from working extra hours, rather than from commanding a higher rate of return on your labour. And this is a common feature of small businesses: often the hourly rate is lousy when compared to employed work — but self-employed people can regulate how much they earn by how many hours they choose to work. And there may be other, non-monetary rewards that go with self-employment.

3. Lifestyle choice

This may be about being able to choose your hours of work or location or the values by which you live your life and conduct your business. Or being able to 'grow' personally by experiencing new challenges and acquiring new skills.

You still have to do the work to make the money and there will still be some drudge elements or unpleasant parts to the job. So lifestyle may be a trade-off. Consider what you are willing to give and what you expect to get in return.

If your motivation is 'convenience' or looking for something which does not interfere too much with your family and social life, you are probably setting yourself up for failure. You will be competing with businesses which are 100 per cent committed; they will prevail.

There are other possible motivations: being made redundant; easing back into work after a break for parenting; no other opportunities around; envy about the daily rates that you see consultants charge. These are not good reasons unless you also have strong positive motivations to reinforce them. This is because there are disadvantages to self-employment, and you need to take into account how comfortable you will be in handling these too.

Here are some of the disadvantages you may need to take into account:

- Long hours
- Poor working conditions
- Loneliness and isolation
- Uncertainty of income
- No holiday pay or sick pay
- No one to 'mind the shop' if you get sick or want to take a break
- Risk of losing your home and other assets if the business folds
- Dealing with people who owe you money
- Having to do everything yourself
- Having to become a salesperson.

The last consideration on the list is an interesting one. It should be obvious, but is overlooked surprisingly often. Yet people are more likely to be motivated by their winning idea, or their skill at making something, than by the prospect of then having to find a buyer.

Changing Careers

But at the end of the day, you have got to sell something to bring in any money!

WHO IS MOST LIKELY TO BECOME SUCCESSFUL IN SELF-EMPLOYMENT?

Obviously you need relevant job-specific technical skills. In addition you will need a range of interpersonal and business skills, such as:

- ☑ Customer service skills
- ☑ Money handling
- ☑ Merchandising/presenting skills
- ☑ Book-keeping skills
- ☑ Negotiating and selling skills
- ☑ Self-promotion skills
- ☑ Self-management skills.

You may also need to have high tolerance to risk and uncertainty and perhaps even loneliness and isolation.

Ultimately, most self-employment situations that fail do so not because of lack of technical ability, but because of temperamental unsuitability. 'Interview' yourself before you choose this option.

SUMMARY

The first part of this chapter covered the challenge of researching where the jobs are and what skills they need. The emphasis is on identifying jobs which use the skills you want to use, rather than on finding familiar job titles.

Next the need to market yourself proactively to avoid the 'cattle market' situations associated with the job advert-application-interview sequence of whittling out competitor applicants was considered.

The CV and interview are inevitably part of your self-presentation, so some hints were given here to maximise impact. The need for self-assessment if self-employment is an option you are considering was also stressed.

ENDNOTE: STRESS MANAGEMENT

Job seeking is the part of the career-change process which is most likely to induce stress. Frustrating dead ends, tense waits, pressures to impress, and sometimes rejections and dashed hopes are all part of the territory. So you will need strong stress-management tactics.

Think in terms of two categories:

1. Your sources of stress/distress (you want to minimise these);
2. Job searching is itself a source of stress.

But stress can be accumulative, so try not to compound the job-search stress by adding other stresses. So, if you can, avoid making other major changes at the same time. And avoid spillover stress, such as moodiness which might contaminate relationships and create new stresses.

Supporting resources help you manage a given stress level. These are your key resources:

1. Internal

Your healthy practices for dealing with stress (exercise, relaxation, balanced use of time, communication, avoidance of dependencies on drugs, alcohol etc.)

> **2. *Fallback plan***
>
> This may be a 'Plan B' if your first goal does not work. It may be the safety net of some 'rainy day' savings that you have put aside. You won't want to use either of these, but knowing they are there can reduce the pressure.
>
> **3. *Other people***
>
> Family and friends can be essential supports. Talk with them and discuss your concerns.
>
> Basically, as long as your coping resources are strong enough to deal with the stress you encounter, then stress is not a problem. Make sure those coping resources are in place for you.

Chapter 8

MAKING THE MOVE

Key ideas in this chapter:
Forcefield analysis
Motivators
Enjoying the Journey

This final chapter urges you to move from *reading* to *doing*. Change doesn't just require ideas, it also requires action. So we will start off with a model of change and the forces motivating in favour of change and those impeding it.

Then a case example will be used to remind you of the processes in this book and to summarise what we have covered. After that, it is over to you.

Forcefield analysis of change and motivators

Change can be scary and uncomfortable. It is not all good and positive, so even if we want change, we may be tempted to put it off.

The diagram that follows considers the two sides of change. It illustrates the forces helping you to change (on the left) and those

Changing Careers

stopping you from changing (on the right). If the forces on the left are stronger than the resisting forces on the right, then you will be propelled to move forward. The stronger those forces, the faster you will go.

Forces helping to motivate for the change ⟹	Forces opposing the change ⟸
Vision Having a clear, compelling vision for what you want to do gives you a target to aim for.	
First steps Once you are moving, it is easier to continue moving. So, identifying a decisive first step, can set you in motion.	**Obstacles** There may be real or perceived barriers in your way. You can de-power these obstacles by identifying them and creating tactics to accommodate them or minimise them.
Dissatisfaction The more clearly dissatisfied you are with the current situation, the greater your incentive to do something about changing it. Harness your dissatisfaction and make it work to your advantage.	

Making the move

Forces helping to motivate for the change ⟹	Forces opposing the change ⟸
Supporting resources The stronger your internal and social support, the better your coping powers to deal with the uncertainty of change.	**Losses** You may have to give up some things in order to change. If you identify the real losses and the risks, you can minimise their effect.
Advantages The more clear you are about the advantages of the change, the more you can draw motivation from this understanding.	

Here is an exercise using this diagram. You can do it on your own with a piece of paper, or in discussion with a person close to you. All you need to do is go down the list and describe as vividly as you can all your visions, plans and other insights about your helpful, motivating forces. And describe what you are going to do to keep the right-hand, restraining forces, in perspective and in check.

Then think about the items on the left-hand side of the chart. Which ones could you make stronger and more helpful to you? And for those on the right, how could you reduce their power and influence on you?

If some of your helpful forces are strong and others not yet fully developed, use the strongest ones to help you. For example, if you don't yet have a clear vision but you do have strong dissatisfaction and you know the first steps, use these to start with. Don't wait until you have 100 per cent certainty about everything. Build up the missing factors as you progress forward.

In some ways, this diagram is a summary of the book:

- ☑ work out your vision: what you want and why you want it;
- ☑ work out your resources (skills, support networks etc);
- ☑ work out your plan and particularly the first concrete actions you need to take;
- ☑ identify your obstacles and risks and create tactics to deal with them.

There are exercises throughout the book to help you implement these steps. But I remind you again that the exercises are designed to *stimulate* your thinking not *constrain* it. You don't need to do all the exercises, and for those that you do complete some will have more value to you than others. Use the ideas presented in this book to help you create your own methodology.

Finally, here is a case example of someone using the techniques. The story is slightly caricatured, but may serve as a quick reminder of the concepts and the processes we have covered in the preceding chapters.

CASE STUDY

Barbara was a mid-level bank officer with an accounting degree. She had been sent along to one of my workshops by her employer in the hope that she would somehow rediscover motivation and direction — or leave the company.

Barbara arrived resentful and bitter that her employer undervalued her skills and experience. The first activity, a lifeline exercise (Diagram 3, page 23) just confirmed her unhappiness. But in combination with the profile of a job (Diagram 1, page 12) it brought home to her the message that she had to do something urgently to fix the problem. If she did not, things would surely get worse and she would be the one to suffer.

She also recognised that the answer was not to look for a similar job 'with a better boss in a better company'. The real problem was that the work no longer excited her. She needed something different.

At this stage she had no clear vision of what she wanted, but she knew she did not want too high a level of responsibility, nor did she want to go back to the bottom of a career ladder. Interesting, stress-free and well-paid work would be nice, thank you.

Barbara produced a mediocre mindmap of her skills (page 31). She struggled to think of any skills outside the ones she used in her current job. The exercise did not seem to be telling her anything new.

But she went home that evening with the job satisfaction model (the three circles on page 14) playing on her mind. At first, she could only think about how little overlap there was between what she enjoyed and what her job needed. But then she mindmapped all the things she enjoyed and the skills that those activities needed. This mindmap was a lot more detailed and imaginative.

At our next meeting she had a long list of skills, both those in her current repertoire and those she wanted to acquire. She did not know where she wanted to use them; they did not correspond to any identifiable job she could think of. We whittled the list down to those that she felt were most essential. These included: creativity, helping people learn, working with people, solving problems, using technology. She also wanted work with variety and work that

Changing Careers

contributed to the community. And she still wanted high pay and seniority and not too much responsibility.

I asked her to think about her 'must have' items and her 'would like to have' items from this list. Deciding on these is as much about what you are willing to give up as what you want to gain. She couldn't decide. Obstacles (page 59) such as family and financial burdens also preyed heavily on her mind.

So next we brainstormed possible jobs (page 83) that could utilise the skills that she wanted to use (assuming we could solve her other concerns). She added to the list over the coming weeks as she was working on other tasks.

Then she set to work finding out about some of the potential jobs. She went to the library; she talked to people she knew; she got on the Internet. Her interest faded quickly for some jobs, but three occupations kept coming back to her: teaching, working with refugee resettlement, and voluntary service overseas.

Each had practical drawbacks. Pay was an issue for all three. Her family obligations would prevent her working overseas at the moment. Her home base was not a major centre for refugees.

But her vision was starting to form. Money and technology were not that important to her. Helping people was. She could see a short-term and a longer-term course of action. In the short term, teaching (possibly accountancy, possibly at high school or polytechnic) was a good option. Later when her children were older, relocation or voluntary overseas aid work held strong appeal, particularly some sort of cross-cultural skill-building work.

The next task was to put together her training plan (pages 54 and 55). The core element was obvious: teacher training. But she also looked at options that would later help to position her to work with other cultures and English as a second language groups.

Making the move

Finally, there was a practical problem to deal with. There would be a loss of income while she attended teachers' college. Her initial plan was to put off the career move for a few years to build up some savings. She also considered some language school jobs where a teacher qualification was not essential.

Then the bank announced a downsizing and asked for volunteers to accept redundancy. Her exit package eased her into the training and into her new career. She suspects that she will not stay in teaching for too many years, but making further career shifts holds no fear for her now.

ENDNOTE: ENJOY YOUR JOURNEY

It is natural that people have some anxiety about change. Often that anxiety causes people to delay changes or to move more cautiously. But it is really common to hear career changes say after the shift: 'I should have done this years earlier.' From the far side of a change, the anxieties, the hurdles and the potential losses look smaller. The new challendes and the spirit of renewal are what matters, they find.

It is quite common for the end goal not to be reached. Your vision changes. The vision improves. Many conclude that it is not the career destination that matters, it is the journey. They make theirs an interesting and varied journey.

Enjoy your journey.